NFL WIDEOUTS

by Craig Ellenport

SCHOLASTIC INC.

No part of this publication may be reproduced, stored in a retrieval system,
or transmitted in any form or by any means, electronic, mechanical, photocopying, recording, or
otherwise, without written permission of the publisher. For information regarding permission, write
to Scholastic Inc., Attention: Permissions Department, 557 Broadway, New York, NY 10012.

ISBN 978-0-545-43494-2

12 11 10 9 8 7 6 5 4 3 2 1   12 13 14 15 16 17/0

Designed by Cheung Tai
Printed in the U.S.A. 40
First printing, September 2012

CONTENTS

VICTOR CRUZ

Cruuuuuuz!" the fans chanted while celebrating the New York Giants' big win over the New England Patriots in the Super Bowl.

That's their way of cheering Giants wide receiver Victor Cruz, which they did an awful lot during the 2011 season. It may be hard to believe, because few of them even knew who Victor Cruz was before last season.

Not even Cruz himself could have expected his sudden rise to stardom.

Cruz actually grew up 15 minutes from where the Giants play in New Jersey. He was good at football, and sports became a way for Cruz to avoid the dangers of the neighborhood where he lived. But the top football colleges didn't think Cruz was big enough. He went to the University of Massachusetts, a school that was not known for sending players to the NFL.

Cruz was the best wideout on his team, but that wasn't enough to get noticed by NFL scouts. No team took him in the 2010 NFL Draft.

After the Draft, the Giants were looking for some additional talent and offered Cruz a chance to sign with them. Cruz knew he had to work twice as hard just to make the team as a backup. His big opportunity to prove himself came in a preseason game against the rival New York Jets. Out of nowhere, Cruz made moves and scored three touchdowns.

The Giants added him to the roster for the regular season. Unfortunately three games into the season he hurt his leg and couldn't play for the rest of the year.

Cruz remained focused on getting better. One day his cell phone rang, and it was none other than Eli Manning! The star quarterback invited Cruz to work out with him. Cruz and Manning became friends after practicing together.

The next season, Cruz was suddenly making big plays. In a Week 3 game against the Eagles, he scored his first career touchdown – a 74-yard bomb. And he never looked back.

By the time the season was over, Cruz set a new Giants record with 1,536 receiving yards. He caught 82 passes and scored 9 touchdowns.

As a tribute to his grandmother, Cruz celebrated his touchdowns by dancing the "salsa," which his grandmother taught him as a kid. The fans went nuts every time Cruz broke into his salsa dance.

Cruz's amazing first full season ended with a trip to the

Super Bowl. Sure enough, he scored the first touchdown of the game and broke into a salsa dance with the whole world watching!

It was an unbelievable way to end a storybook season.

A.J. GREEN

Most experts agree that it's pretty hard to be a dominating wide receiver in your first NFL season. It usually takes a year or two to develop into a superstar. It takes time to learn all the different plays that are run in the NFL.

Apparently, nobody told A.J. Green that he wasn't supposed to be an NFL star right away. When he joined the Cincinnati Bengals in 2011, he became the first rookie wideout to make the Pro Bowl in eight years!

It wasn't a complete surprise. People knew that Green would be great. That's why the Bengals selected him with the fourth overall pick in the 2011 Draft. He was the first receiver taken in the Draft. Green was one of the top receivers in the country during his first year at the University of Georgia.

Green was considered a "can't-miss" NFL prospect. He was smart, fast, and had good size for the position – 6 feet, 4 inches tall and 207 pounds. He was also very good at leaping, so he could out-jump defensive players for high passes.

One other quality stood out: Green had excellent hand-eye coordination. In other words, he was very good at seeing where the football was going and quickly putting his hands in the right position to make a catch. Green got his hand-eye coordination from juggling. He learned to juggle when he was in second grade and, before long, he was able to juggle four balls at once! In the fourth grade, he learned how to ride a unicycle. The balance that it takes to ride a unicycle also helped him when it came to twisting, diving, and lunging to catch footballs.

Still, with all the skills Green brought with him to the Bengals, few could have predicted he would be so good so fast. After all, the Bengals' offense was going through major changes. For many years, they were led by the combination of quarterback Carson Palmer and receiver Chad Ochocinco. But neither of those players was on the team in 2011.

Green made an immediate impact when he replaced Ochocinco. In his first game for the Bengals, he only caught one pass — but it was a 41-yard touchdown in the fourth quarter that gave Cincinnati the lead. The Bengals went on to win that game, and they finished the season with a 9-7 record and made the playoffs.

Green finished the season with 65 catches for 1,057 yards and 7 touchdowns. It was an impressive start to what should be a very promising career.

GREG JENNINGS

I t's better to give than to receive," is one of the important values Greg Jennings learned growing up as the son of a church pastor. Off the football field, Jennings always keeps that expression in mind and uses his position as a famous athlete to help others. On the field, however, Jennings has found that it is much better to receive!

When Jennings joined the Green Bay Packers as their big-play receiver, he quickly became a favorite target of legendary quarterback Brett Favre. But when Aaron Rodgers took Favre's place, the Packers' offense didn't miss a beat – and Jennings had a lot to do with that.

Growing up in Kalamazoo, Michigan, Jennings actually played four different positions in high school: receiver, running back, outside linebacker, and defensive back. When he got to college at Western Michigan University, he focused on being a receiver. He became the eleventh player in college football history to record at least 1,000 receiving yards in a season three times. He caught the eye of NFL scouts, and the Packers took Jennings in the second round of the 2006 draft.

That summer, Jennings made such a good impression on the coaching staff that he became a starter in his first game. Just a few weeks into his rookie season, he showed he could be counted on to make big plays when he caught a 75-yard touchdown pass. This play was the first of several times that Jennings helped his teammate Brett Favre make NFL history.

Aaron Rodgers took over for Favre as the Packers QB in 2008, but Jennings had no trouble adjusting to a new quarterback. In fact, he went on to record three straight seasons with at least 1,000 receiving yards. And when the Packers made it to the Super Bowl after the 2010 season, Jennings caught 2 touchdown passes in their Super Bowl XLV win over the Pittsburgh Steelers.

Jennings earned his first Pro Bowl trip after the 2010 season, and he is now regarded as one of the best receivers in the NFL. But Jennings is interested in much more than football. He's appeared as an actor on a few television shows, and he always works hard with his foundation to help people in need.

After all, it is better to give than receive. Off the field, at least.

CALVIN JOHNSON

When Calvin Johnson was growing up as a kid in Newnan, Georgia, his parents taught him the importance of working hard. Johnson has always worked very hard at his football career. But when you combine that hard work with Johnson's unbelievable size and athletic ability, that's what makes him a superstar.

Johnson was already 6 feet tall in middle school, and 6 feet, 4 inches tall by the time he was in tenth grade. In addition to being taller than most wide receivers, he was also faster than most, with big hands to catch the football and very good hand-eye coordination. Because of all that, Johnson was always making big plays.

Football came easily to Johnson. He was a star in high school, and he was named one of the top players in the country before choosing to play football for

19

Georgia Tech University. In three years at Georgia Tech, he set school records and was looked at as a top NFL prospect.

Even though the Detroit Lions had drafted receivers with their first-round pick in 2003, 2004, and 2005, they couldn't pass up the chance to take Johnson with the second overall pick in the 2007 Draft.

It didn't take long for Johnson to show what he could do in the NFL. He caught a touchdown pass in his first game as a Lion. Overall, he finished his rookie season with 48 receptions for 756 yards and he scored 5 total touchdowns.

Roy Williams, one of the other first-round wideouts on the Lions, was so impressed with Johnson's incredible size and ability that he gave him the nickname "Megatron," referring to the dangerous robot in the Transformers movies.

Even though everybody knew that Johnson was an incredible player, he never stopped working and practicing. He continued to get better every season. As a result, the Lions – a team that had not been to the playoffs in eight years – also continued to get better.

It took a little longer for the team to get better though. In 2008, the Lions became the first NFL team ever to finish with a record of 0-16. However, Johnson caught 78 passes for 1,331 yards, and he led the NFL with 12 TD catches.

In 2010, Johnson was named to the Pro Bowl for the first time. And in 2011, just as the Lions were ready to finally become a playoff team, Johnson showed everyone how good he could be. Surprisingly the Lions got off to a 4-0 start, and Johnson tied an NFL record by catching 2 TD passes in each of those four games. By the time the season ended, the Lions had made it to their first playoff game in 12 years and Johnson set career highs for catches (96), yards (1,681), and touchdowns (16).

Megatron might be a villain in the movies, but he's a superhero for the Lions!

MIKE WALLACE

In the grand history of the Pittsburgh Steelers, there have been some terrific wideouts, like Hall of Famers Lynn Swann and John Stallworth, and MVP Hines Ward.

Still, after just three seasons, Mike Wallace could be on his way to becoming the best receiver in Steelers history.

Not bad for a kid who once relied only on his great speed. Wallace has since learned that it takes more than being fast to succeed in the NFL.

Speed seemed like it would be enough when Wallace was growing up in New Orleans, Louisiana. He was a backup on his football team until the coach decided to let his fastest player return kicks. All Wallace did that season was return 4 punts for touchdowns and 4 kickoffs for touchdowns – and he had 7 more

touchdown returns that were called back because of penalties!

After a successful college career at the University of Mississippi, it was time for Wallace to go to the NFL Scouting Combine. That's where college players from around the country gather for scouts from all the NFL teams. They are tested for speed, strength, and other athletic talents. And again, Wallace's speed was the story. He ran the 40-yard dash in 4.33 seconds – the second-fastest time among all the receivers at the Combine.

But he wasn't the second receiver taken in the Draft that year. He was the eleventh receiver taken – and not until the third round. Another reminder that he needed more than just speed to be a star in the NFL.

Still, speed did help. Wallace caught 39 passes for 756 yards and scored 6 touchdowns as a rookie. He had a great average – more than 19 yards per reception. In his second season, Wallace topped that. He caught 60 passes for 1,257 yards – an average of nearly 21 yards per catch – with 10 touchdowns.

Even the Steelers' head coach, Mike Tomlin, used to joke that Wallace was a "one-trick pony" – that he just did one thing well, which was trying to outrun

the defense and let quarterback Ben Roethlisberger throw it as far as he could.

In 2011, Wallace worked harder to expand his game. Instead of trying to outrun the defense on long passes, he caught shorter passes – and then outran the defense. It worked. Wallace had more than 100 yards receiving in each of the first three games of the season. And by the end of the season, Wallace earned his first trip to the Pro Bowl.

"I guess I'm not a one-trick guy anymore," said Wallace.

WES WELKER

In five seasons with the New England Patriots, Wes Welker has become one of the best wide receivers in the NFL. He is a favorite target of quarterback Tom Brady, and he has set many team and league records. It has been an amazing journey for a player who was always considered too small to succeed.

Actually, being too small is one of the reasons Welker became so good in the first place. He grew up playing football with his older brother and his friends, so he was always the smallest kid on the field. This only

made him try harder. By the time he got to high school, he was ready for anything – and he did everything. Welker starred on offense, defense, and special teams. He once kicked a 58-yard field goal, something many kickers in the NFL have never done!

Welker earned player of the year honors in Oklahoma as a high school senior, but that didn't matter when it came to playing at the next level. He didn't get any scholarship offers to play at a major college football program. Welker knew it was because he was only 5 feet, 9 inches tall, and most coaches thought that was too small to succeed as a running back or wideout. Welker was upset about not getting a chance. Finally, there was a last-minute opening at Texas Tech University, and Welker made the best of it.

Welker was moved to wide receiver at Texas Tech. He excelled both as a receiver and a punt returner. But it didn't help convince anyone he was big enough to do well at the professional level. Welker was not selected by any team in the 2004 NFL Draft.

Determined to prove them wrong, he signed to be a backup for the San Diego Chargers. But he played only one game for the Chargers before they cut him. The Miami Dolphins signed him after that, but he was still regarded as more of a special-teams player.

However, at least one important NFL coach took notice. Welker always seemed to play well against Miami's

AFC East Division rival, the New England Patriots. Bill Belichick, coach of the Patriots, traded for Welker before the 2007 season.

To say that Welker was a perfect fit for the Patriots is an understatement. After catching a total of 96 passes and scoring just 1 touchdown in his first four seasons in the NFL, Welker caught 112 passes for 8 touchdowns in 2007 alone! The Patriots had one of the most explosive, high-scoring offenses in NFL history, and Welker was suddenly a big part of that.

Once he finally proved he could be a star at the highest level, Welker never stopped working hard. He stills plays well for New England, catching more than 100 passes in four of his five seasons with the Patriots and being selected to play in the Pro Bowl four times.